KNOW IT

LIFE CYCLES

By Louise Nel

BookLife
PUBLISHING

©This edition published in 2022.
First published in 2021.
BookLife Publishing Ltd.
King's Lynn
Norfolk, PE30 4LS, UK

A catalogue record for this book is available from the British Library.

ISBN: 978-1-80155-577-7

All facts, statistics, web addresses and URLs in this book were verified as valid and accurate at time of writing. No responsibility for any changes to external websites or references can be accepted by either the author or publisher.

Written by:
Louise Nelson

Edited by:
John Wood

Designed by:
Dan Scase

PHOTO CREDITS

All images are courtesy of Shutterstock.com. With thanks to Getty Images, Thinkstock Photo and iStockphoto. Front cover: irin-k, Leptospira, Smit, Mirek Kijewski, Javi Roces, Potapov Alexander, suns07butterfly, Olhastock, Pineapple studio, PixaHub, Ian 2010, Eric Isselee. Page 1 – suns07butterfly. 4&5 – Minerva Studio, Jiri Hera, Jacek Chabraszewski, Hogan Imaging, Tom Wang, Butterfly Hunter, kdshutterman, Krakenimages.com, Amy Lutz, VaLiza. 6&7 – 5 second Studio, Marlonneke Willemsen, Narupon Nimpaiboon, Vangert, Dirk Ercken, Eric Isselee, andersphoto, Valentyna Chukhlyebova, Moon Light PhotoStudio, P. OCHASANOND, Nejron Photo, Tsekhmister, kirillov alexey. 8&9 – canadastock, Chansom Pantip, Khudoliy, Eric Isselee, Ken C Moore, Rebecca Schreiner. 10&11 – Artiste2d3d, Zerbor, Olga Shpak, Smileus, Patryk Kosmider, stockphoto mania, photomaster, Willyam Bradberry, gualtiero boffi, Daria Rybakova, KF2017, Alexey Seafarer, Eric Isselee, Jennifer White Maxwell, Nantawat Chotsuwan, Ondrej Prosicky, Subbotina Anna, KangGod. 12&13 – scubaluna, Andres Sonne, Ermolaev Alexander, dragon_fang, Matt Jeppson, Ihor Hvozdetskyi, Solodov Aleksei, JoLin, yevgeniy11, Photoongraphy, Roger Clark ARPS, Rich Carey. 14&15 – IrinaK, Independent birds, pandapaw, Oleksandr Lytvynenko, Carlos E. Santa Maria, Eric Isselee, Evgeny Dubinchuk, gracious_tiger. 16&17 – Tim UR, Elvan, David Carillet, Ian 2010, Zephyris, Ethan Daniels, Levent Konuk. 18&19 – Oleksandr Lytvynenko, Eric Isselee, Imagine Earth Photography, Smileus, Eric Isselee, Anders Riishede, ESB Professional, domnitsky, Africa Studio, Kletr, LilKar, Fotofermer. 20&21 – Mathisa, Thammanoon Khamchalee, K Hanley CHDPhoto, Cathy Keifer, hwongcc, hwongcc, Robert Ross. 22&23 – Eric Isselee, Sergey Uryadnikov, Albert Beukhof, Mike Laptev, WildlifeWorld, Natalia Khalaman. 24&25 – Eric Isselee, abcphotosystem, CAPE COCONUT, Elena Elisseeva, Shebeko, Sakss, Nella. 26&27 – Arcaion, Ihor Hvozdetskyi. schankz, Protasov AN, Zheltyshev, Kuttelvaserova Stuchelova, Sergei25, Eldred Lim, Anita Kainrath. 28&29 – Eric Isselee, withGod, anat chant, Chepko Danil Vitalevich, Jürgen Otto, Protasov AN, Lukiyanova Natalia frenta, Iakov Filimonov, NuntekulPhotography. 30&31 – Eric Isselee, absolutimages, Tony Campbell, Antonio Gravante, Csanad Kiss, piccatcher, irin-k, DenisNata, stockphoto mania, yevgeniy11. 32&33 – Smileus, Richard Peterson, DMITRY KOROBEYNIKOV, Benny Marty, Mark_Kostich, Luke Shelley, Svetlana Foote, Nancy Bauer, Landshark1, Andy Reago & Chrissy McClarren. 34&35 – NeiraStudios, Rosa Jay, jps, Eric Isselee, schankz, Vladimir Melnik, WildlifeWorld, Tsekhmister, Eoghan, yevgeniy11, Dolores M. Harvey, Daria Rybakova, Ryzhkov Sergey, Sebastian Janicki, Tatyana Vyc. 36&37 – stscheb, CLS Digital Arts.

CONTENTS

Page 4   **Living Things**

Page 6   **Key Ideas**

Page 8   **The Journey Through Life**

Page 10   **Timeline: Life Spans**

Page 12   **Eggs**

Page 14   **Pregnancy**

Page 16   **Seeds**

Page 18   **Offspring**

Page 20   **Metamorphosis**

Page 22   **Juveniles**

Page 28   **Adulthood**

Page 30   **The Life Cycle**

Page 32   **Believe It or Not!**

Page 34   **Activities**

Page 36   **Quick Quizzes**

Page 38   **Glossary**

Page 40   **Index**

**Words that look like <u>this</u> can be found in the glossary on page 38.
Key ideas you will need can be found on page 6.**

LIVING THINGS

You are a living thing. So are animals and plants. This book is not a living thing. It cannot eat, move or grow. A dry leaf on the ground was once part of a living thing, but it is no longer living. Now it is dead.

LIVING

NOT LIVING

Living things breathe, eat, grow, move, **reproduce** and get rid of **waste**. Living things also use their **senses.**

GROW

EAT

REPRODUCE

BREATHE

MOVE

4

All lives have a beginning, a middle, and an end. All living things start off small and young. They grow and change, and have **offspring** of their own. They will grow old. Eventually, all living things will die. Every living thing will follow this path through life, and this is called the life cycle.

NO LONGER LIVING

PARENT

GRANDPARENT

CHILD

5

KEY IDEAS

LIFE ON EARTH

Animals are living things. They can usually move around by themselves, and they need food and water to live. Here is a list of some types of animals!

A gecko is a **reptile**.

A frog is an **amphibian**.

An ant is an **insect**.

A parrot is a bird.

A goldfish is a fish.

A cat is a **mammal**.

PLANTS

Plants are living things. Most have roots in the ground and don't move around. They can also have leaves, fruit and tubers. Plants can be flowering or non-flowering.

A strawberry plant is a flowering plant.

A tree is a flowering plant. This is a willow tree.

Ferns and mosses are non-flowering plants.

A rose is a flowering plant.

WHAT IS REPRODUCTION?

All living things need to make more of themselves so that their **species** carries on. These new individuals are called offspring. Most living things need a male and a female to reproduce.

Baby chickens are called chicks.

Young dogs are called puppies.

New plants are called seedlings.

DID YOU KNOW?

All living things can **sense** the world around them.

7

THE JOURNEY THROUGH LIFE

All living things have a life span. This is the usual amount of time they will probably live. Life spans can be very short or very long.

Sierra redwood trees can have a life span of around 3,500 years.

English ivy can have a life span of around 440 years.

You can tell how old a tree is by counting the rings that run through its trunk.

Marigold plants have a life span of less than a year.

Some life cycles might only last for a few hours or days, while others last for hundreds of years.

The bowhead whale has a very long life span. It can live for up to 200 years.

The mayfly has a short life span. Their adult life only lasts for 24 hours.

The immortal jellyfish is very special because it doesn't get old. If it gets attacked or injured, it can turn back into a baby and start again.

Living things take the same journey through life. First, they are born. They are young, and they grow into adults. Most of them will reproduce. They will grow older, and eventually their life span will end.

HYACINTH (PLANT)

DID YOU KNOW?

It is thought that the oldest human ever was Jeanne Louise Calment. She was born in France in 1875 and died in 1997 at the age of 122 years old.

TIMELINE: LIFE SPANS

Bristlecone
pine tree
4,900 years

English oak tree
1,500 years

Bowhead whale
200 years

Rhinoceros
40 years

Donkey
40–50 years

**Cottonmouth
snake**
24 years

Emperor penguin
20 years

Cat
14 years

Grizzly bear
25 years

Mayfly
24 hours

Housefly
4 weeks

Galápagos giant tortoise
150 years

Macaw
60 years

Laysan albatross
65 years

African elephant
70 years

Bullfrog
7–9 years

Seahorse
6 years

Guinea pig
5 years

Hummingbird
3–5 years

Dragonfly
4 months

Chameleon
3 years

EGGS

Many animals, including birds, reptiles and insects, lay eggs. First, the female will find a mate who will **fertilise** her eggs. She will then lay her eggs on the ground, with the offspring growing inside them. Fish eggs are often soft and jelly-like. Bird eggs have a hard shell. Reptile eggs can have a soft shell.

Turtles lay their soft, round eggs in nests they dig on the beach.

Most fish lay a lot of small eggs in water.

Ostrich eggs are very large!

Bee eggs are laid inside special wax cells. The eggs look like tiny grains of rice.

Most birds lay their eggs in nests.

Robins' eggs are small and bright blue.

Male penguins look after the eggs. They keep the eggs on their feet to keep them warm.

Inside the egg, the new offspring will grow. An egg gives the offspring all the food it needs. Some animals will stay with their eggs to protect them from **predators** and keep them warm. Other animals will lay their eggs and then leave, without looking after them at all.

Mother hens sit on their eggs to keep them warm.

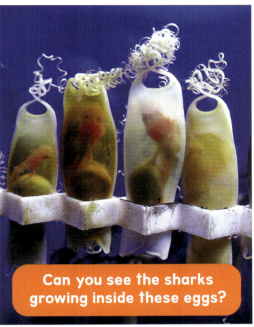

Can you see the sharks growing inside these eggs?

For seahorses, it is the male who carries the eggs in his body.

Crocodiles are good parents and will often guard their nests fiercely!

This squid is almost ready to hatch from its egg.

DID YOU KNOW?

A group of eggs laid by a mother is called a clutch. Some animals lay millions of eggs in a clutch – others lay just one!

PREGNANCY

Mammals don't usually lay eggs. The offspring of mammals grow inside the mother's **uterus**. Her body gives it all the food it needs. The amount of time a mammal is pregnant is called gestation, and it is different for each species. Some mammals usually have just one offspring, while others can have many more.

The Virginian opossum is pregnant for just 12 days.

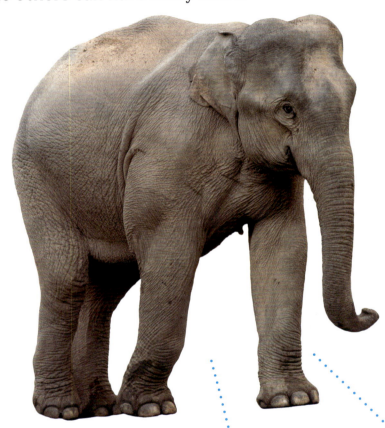

Cats are pregnant for around 65 days and can have around five kittens in a litter.

Indian elephants are pregnant for around 22 months – that's almost two years!

Zebras are pregnant for 11–12 months. Can you see this female's swollen belly? That's the baby inside!

Human mothers are pregnant for around nine months.

14

The mother will give birth to her offspring. This means she will push them out of her body. Some offspring are very small and helpless when they are born, and they will need a lot of care and time to grow. Other offspring can stand, run and drink their mother's milk soon after being born.

Newborn cows are called calves. They can stand, walk and feed on their own just one hour after being born.

Newborn rats are born with no fur and with their eyes closed. They are very **vulnerable**.

Giraffe mothers give birth standing up. Their baby falls almost two metres to the ground! This doesn't hurt them – but it does help them take their first big breath. The baby can walk on its own in an hour.

DID YOU KNOW?

Usually, smaller animals are pregnant for short periods of time, and bigger animals are pregnant for longer.

Kittens (baby cats) are born with their eyes and ears closed.

SEES

Some plants start life as seeds. Seeds are made inside flowers, fruit or cones. Seeds need to leave the parent plant and find a good place to grow into new plants. Seeds can be carried away from the plant by wind, water or animals.

CONE

Tomato seeds are found inside its bright red fruit.

Sunflower seeds can be found here, in the centre of the flower.

Birds eat seeds and then fly away. The seeds come out later in their <u>droppings</u>.

Can you see the seeds tucked into this pinecone?

SEEDS

Coconut seeds float away on the water, and grow when they land on the beach.

Spiky seeds are called burrs. They are covered in tiny hooks, which get stuck on furry animals. The animal carries the burr away to a place to grow.

Dandelion seeds are carried away by the wind.

GERMINATION

Seeds need water, air and the right temperature to grow. When these **conditions** are right, the seed will put out tiny roots and a small stalk called a shoot. The shoot will grow small leaves. This is called germination. Plants all do this differently, but the basic **process** is the same.

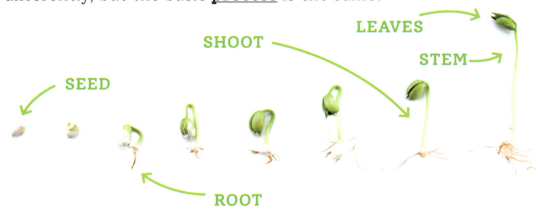

LEAVES

SHOOT

STEM

SEED

ROOT

DID YOU KNOW?

Tomatoes are actually a fruit! Fruit is the part of a plant that carries the seeds, so if you see seeds, you're looking at a fruit!

17

OFFSPRING

ANIMAL OFFSPRING

Some animal offspring quickly look like smaller **versions** of their parents. These small animals will be vulnerable to predators. Some parents protect their offspring, carrying them around and feeding them. Other babies have to look after themselves. These animals often have very good **camouflage** to hide them from predators.

Cat and kitten

Mother kangaroos carry their offspring in a pouch.

This baby baboon looks up at its mother.

This mother horse. called a mare. is the same colour as her foal.

A leopard gecko climbs on its mother's back.

This is a mother humpback whale and her calf. Humpbacks call each other with amazing songs. and calves are known to whisper to their mothers.

You might look just like one of your parents. or a mixture of the two.

PLANT OFFSPRING

Leaves come out of the plant's shoot. The roots of the plant will take in **nutrients**, and the leaves will take in sunlight and a **gas** called carbon dioxide. These things make food for the plant to grow. As the plant grows, it will start to look more like its parent plant.

A young <u>citrus</u> tree

A young pea plant

A young tomato plant

Even giant oak trees...

... start off as young seedlings!

DID YOU KNOW?

The plant uses sunlight and carbon dioxide in the air to make food. This is called photosynthesis.

METAMORPHOSIS

LIFE CYCLE OF A BUTTERFLY

Some animal offspring don't look anything like their parents when they are born or hatch from their eggs. These creatures have a special trick: metamorphosis. They will be born in one body, and then when they have eaten enough to grow, they will change their bodies completely to become like the parent.

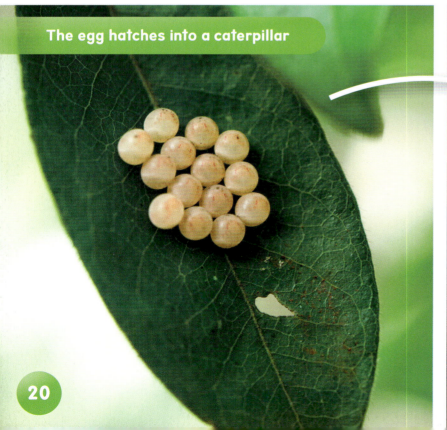

The egg hatches into a caterpillar

The caterpillar eats, and eats… and eats! It grows and grows. As it grows, it loses its skin. This is called moulting.

When it is big enough. the caterpillar will hang upside down from a safe spot. usually a leaf or a branch.

The caterpillar becomes a pupa. In this stage. the caterpillar breaks down its body. Slowly. it grows legs. wings and a body.

The caterpillar splits its old skin. wriggles out. then rests while its new. soft skin hardens.

When the butterfly comes out. its wings will be soft at first. It will need to rest in the sun to let them dry.

Finally. the wings will harden and the transformation is complete! The caterpillar has turned into a butterfly. Its long. soft body has changed. Now it has six legs. wings and a body with antennae. When its wings harden. it can fly away and look for food.

ANTENNAE

SIX LEGS

WINGS

JUVENILES

MAMMALS

Young mammals will stay with their mothers and drink their milk until they are ready to feed themselves. Then they will **wean** and are known as juveniles.

This German shepherd dog is a juvenile. He is not quite a puppy, and not quite an adult.

Juvenile tigers must learn to hunt – so they start with jumping and pouncing!

Juvenile mammals tend to look like adults, but smaller. They are not yet ready to have offspring of their own.

A young wolf

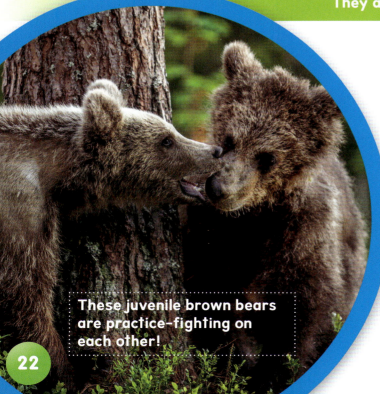

These juvenile brown bears are practice-fighting on each other!

Juvenile animals need to learn about **social rules**, and will often play-fight, testing their strength. They will learn all the skills they need to survive from their parents.

BIRDS

Young birds leave the nest and learn to fly. At this stage, the bird is called a fledgling. As it grows, it will moult its feathers and its adult colours will come through.

A young peregrine falcon

Juvenile birds must learn to fly.

Juvenile penguins, like this yellow-eyed penguin, moult their fluffy feathers, which kept them warm as babies.

This fledgling barn owl has some of its adult feathers, but still has some of its fluffy baby feathers too.

DID YOU KNOW?

Juvenile animals will still be smaller than adults, but larger than babies. They will eat and sleep a lot – all that growing is hard work!

REPTILES

Most reptiles grow quickly as juveniles. As they grow, many juvenile reptiles will shed their skin. This is called moulting. Some shed it all in one piece, forming a new, soft skin underneath. Others will shed their skins in small pieces a bit at a time.

Juvenile sea turtles spend up to ten years out at sea before becoming adults. Scientists often call this 'the lost years'.

This rattlesnake has shed its old skin as it has grown.

Juvenile saltwater crocodiles have patterns of dark stripes and spots. These fade out as they become adults.

PLANTS

If conditions are right, juvenile plants can rapidly grow and will soon reach **maturity**. Young trees are called saplings. Saplings have a slim, **flexible** trunk and are between half a metre and three metres tall. Usually, saplings are not ready to make fruit or have flowers. They still have a lot of growing to do!

This maple tree sapling has a thin trunk.

Pine tree saplings have bright green, needle-like juvenile leaves.

This lemon tree sapling has already got a tangle of roots. The roots take in water and nutrients to help the sapling grow. It doesn't have any lemons on it yet.

Sunflower plants start to develop a bud at the top as they grow.

INSECTS

Most insects begin life as eggs. Some simple insects, such as silverfish, look like small adults straight away. Other insects may go through a metamorphosis stage, like the butterfly on page 20. The juvenile might be so different that it has its own name! During metamorphosis, the juvenile is called a pupa.

Gypsy moth

Silverfish

This is a maggot. After moulting a few times. it will enter the pupa stage before becoming a housefly.

The juvenile dragonfly is called a nymph. The nymph lives in the water. then crawls out and goes through its metamorphosis into an adult. Can you see the dragonfly coming out of the body of the nymph?

The bark beetle starts off as an egg, then becomes a larva. The larva has no legs. It goes through metamorphosis as a pupa and grows legs, wings and a hard **exoskeleton**.

FISH

After the egg stage, many fish also become larvae. Larvae still have the yolk from their egg attached. They grow into fry when they can eat on their own. Fry are usually less than one year old. The fish then grow and develop as juveniles. Juveniles are not ready to have offspring of their own.

Fish larva with yolk sac attached

These spanner barb fish are juveniles. They look like small versions of the adult fish.

This is a juvenile lemon shark.

DID YOU KNOW?

Bees all start off as eggs. Worker bees feed the growing larvae. If they need to make a new queen bee, one larva is fed a special food, called royal jelly. When the bees emerge, the queen bee will be much larger than the others!

DID YOU KNOW?

Juvenile predators, such as dolphins, learn to hunt for food.

ADULTHOOD

When an animal or plant is ready to reproduce and have offspring of its own, it is an adult. Some living things will continue to grow throughout their lives, and others will stop growing when they reach adulthood. Adults will be completely independent. This means they can feed themselves, protect themselves, and know what they have to do.

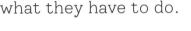
TALONS

Adult predators, such as this golden eagle, develop all the weapons they need. Can you see the sharp talons?

Adult male lions have long, shaggy fur around their heads. This is called a mane.

Adults develop their full colours too, like this wood-boring beetle.

This adult Merino sheep has grown long, curly horns.

The adult feathers of birds are not fluffy like the feathers of babies and juveniles. Once the bird has its adult feathers, it will be able to swim or fly (or maybe both) and become independent.

Adult animals look for a mate so they can make offspring of their own. Many animals show off with their strength, intelligence or beauty to prove that they are the best. Some animals only meet up with others to mate, and then they leave. Others will keep the same mate for life.

The male peacock spider is tiny – but that doesn't stop it putting on a big display! The male will display his colourful crest. and shake it back and forth in a dance to prove to the female that he will be a good mate.

The male peafowl. known as a peacock. displays his impressive tail to find a mate.

Fiddler crabs have one large claw and one small. They use the larger one when fighting other males over a female.

Swans are birds that sometimes mate for life.

Some adult plants produce flowers. Flowers attract bees and other insects. who feed on the flowers and help __pollinate__ the plant.

THE LIFE CYCLE

All living things have a life cycle. Some only live for a short time and some for a very long time. Most living things start off small, as an egg or a seed, or inside a female. Living things grow and change. Some even go through an amazing metamorphosis. When the living thing can feed and protect itself, it is a juvenile.

THE LIFE CYCLE OF A FROG

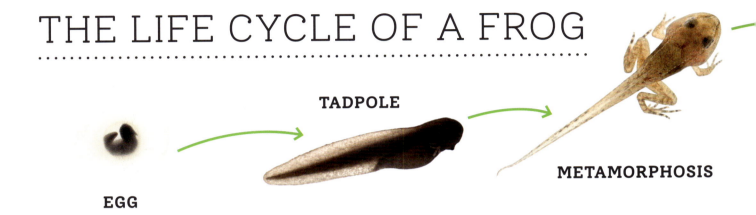

TADPOLE

METAMORPHOSIS

EGG

THE LIFE CYCLE OF A CAT

PREGNANCY

NEWBORN KITTEN

GROWING AND CHANGING

THE LIFE CYCLE OF A CHICKEN

EGG

CHICK

GROWING AND CHANGING

When it is fully grown and ready to have offspring of its own, it is an adult. Adults have all the **features** of their species, and most will reproduce, creating new offspring and continuing the life cycle again. This is the life cycle.

FROGLET

ADULT FROG

JUVENILE

ADULT CAT

JUVENILE

ADULT CHICKEN

DID YOU KNOW?

In the end, all living things will grow old. Eventually, they will die, and the life cycle will be complete.

BELIEVE IT OR NOT!

Let's take a look at some weird and wonderful facts about life cycles.

Kangaroos are only pregnant for around four weeks. The baby joey is born very small and <u>underdeveloped.</u> The tiny baby crawls into a pouch on its mother and grows there. Animals that have this special pouch are called marsupials.

The largest litter of rabbits ever recorded was 24! Rabbits usually have around six babies.

Gorilla mothers often carry their babies on their backs. They can climb and swing while the babies hold on.

The female kiwi bird lays an egg that is half of her body weight!

Female black widow spiders can be very grumpy partners! The female is bigger than the male. and sometimes she eats him!

Birds and some reptiles build nests to keep their eggs safe. Some build amazing nests with decorations. The male bower bird must build an impressive nest to attract a female, so he decorates his nest with brightly coloured things he finds to impress her.

Orcas have long pregnancies. A female orca can be pregnant for 17 to 18 months. She will only have one baby, called a calf.

The woolly bear moth lives in the cold **Arctic**, where there isn't enough food to go through metamorphosis in just one summer. So, this moth lets itself freeze, and waits for the Sun to return. Once it is warm enough, it **thaws** and carries on eating until the weather gets cold and it freezes again. It can do this for up to seven years until it can build a cocoon. Finally, it comes out of the cocoon as a moth in the summer. It mates and lays its own eggs, and then dies after only two weeks of adult life.

ACTIVITIES

Can you complete these fun activities?

ARE YOU MY MUMMY?

Can you match the baby to the mother? Check back through the book if you aren't sure.

a. Kitten

b. Cub

c. Caterpillar

d. Chick

f. Maggot

e. Lamb

g. Pup

h. Chick

i. Piglet

1. Ewe

2. Cat

3. Pig

4. Harp seal

5. Brown bear

6. Saker falcon

7. Swallowtail butterfly

8. Housefly

9. Hen

OUT AND ABOUT

Can you grow a plant from a seed and watch what happens? You could take a photo of your plant every day, or write down what you see in a journal.

QUICK QUIZZES

Can you beat our terrific tests? 3... 2... 1... GO!

WHAT'S MY NAME?

Can you remember the names to answer the questions? Check back through the book if you're not sure.

1. Name the creature that is only alive as an adult for 24 hours.

2. What name do we use for a baby cat?

3. Name the oldest human being ever.

4. Name three types of animal that lay eggs.

5. Larvae turn into pupae. Pupae turn into adults... but what's the name of this transformation?

POP QUIZ QUESTION!

Can you name all seven signs of life?

Check **page 4** for the answer!

Answers: 1. Mayfly. 2. Kitten. 3. Jeanne Louise Calment. 4. Birds, reptiles and fish. 5. Metamorphosis.

PLANT OR ANIMAL?

Can you tell the difference? Check the Key Ideas on page 6 if you need a reminder!

Crocodile

Hyacinth

Tomato

Sunflower

Gecko

Spider

Oak

Teenager

Snake

GLOSSARY

A

amphibian an animal that can live both on land and in water

Arctic part of the cold, icy areas around the North Pole

C

camouflage traits that allow an animal to hide itself in a habitat

citrus a group of plants and fruit, such as oranges, lemons and limes

conditions the state of the environment, such as the temperature, rainfall and food available

D

droppings poo

E

exoskeleton the hard structure on the outside of a creature

F

features interesting or important parts

fertilise make an egg able to create new life

flexible easy to bend

G

gas a thing that is like air, which spreads out to fill any space available

I

insect a very small animal with six legs, a body split into three parts and usually two sets of wings

L

litter a group of babies

M

mammal an animal that has warm blood, a backbone and produces milk

maturity the stage when a living thing is an adult

N

nutrients things that plants and animals need to grow and stay healthy

O

offspring the young of an animal or plant

P

pollinate to pass on pollen from a plant to another plant of the same kind, so that seeds will be produced

predators animals that eat other animals

process a set of steps that happen in an order to get something done

R

reproduce when living things create offspring together

reptile a cold-blooded animal with scales

S

sense to feel or be aware of

senses ways of taking in information about the world, such as seeing and hearing

social rules rules that help animals get along and work together

species a group of very similar animals or plants that can create young together

T

thaws warms up and becomes no longer frozen

U

underdeveloped not fully formed or built

uterus the fluid-filled sac that some babies grow in

V

versions new or different forms of something that already exists

vulnerable being easy to attack or harm

W

waste wee and poo

wean slowly get a baby to eat something other than its mother's milk

INDEX

B
babies 7, 9, 14–15, 18, 23, 28, 32–34, 36
birds 6, 12, 16, 23, 28–29, 32–33
burrs 17

C
camouflage 18
children 5
cocoons 33

E
eggs 12–14, 20, 26–27, 30, 32–33, 36

F
female 7, 12, 14, 29–30, 32–33
ferns 7
fish 6, 12, 27
fledglings 23
flowers 7, 16, 25, 29
fry 27

G
germination 17
grandparents 5

I
insects 6, 12, 26, 29

J
juveniles 22–28, 30–31

L
larvae 27, 36
leaves 4, 7, 17, 19, 21, 25
life spans 8–11
litters 14, 32

M
male 7, 12–13, 28–29, 32–33
mammals 6, 14, 22
marsupials 32
mating 12, 29, 33
metamorphosis 20, 26–27, 30, 33
milk 15, 22
mosses 7
moulting 20, 23–24, 26

N
newborns 15, 30

O
offspring 5, 7, 12–15, 18–20, 22, 27–29, 31

P
parents 5, 13, 16, 18–20, 22
pinecones 17
predators 13, 18, 27–28
pregnancy 14–15, 30, 32–33

R
reproduction 4, 7, 9, 28, 31
reptiles 6, 12, 24, 33
roots 7, 17, 19, 25
royal jelly 27

S
saplings 25
seeds 16–17, 30, 35
shoots 17, 19
species 7, 14, 31
stems 17

T
trees 7–8, 10, 19, 25
trunks 8, 25